Alegmi M. Sofia
Publications
(Hasafa)

The *BIG*-*KNOT*
Book

Human Relationship
with Existence and Life

(A window to Islamic Philosophy)

First Print 2014

BY
Alegmi M. Sofia

Rights

* The Big-Knot book ISBN: **978-9959-1-1319-1**
  - Receipt No: 653/ 2013, Date: December 5 2013
    National books Library, Libya – Benghazi.
  - Email: nat-lib-libya@hotmail.com
   - www.nll.org.ly

----

www.alsofia.net
alsofia@alsofia.net
For Post: Po. Box 122 (Maidan Aljazayer Post), Tripoli -
Libya.
Emails: ajmisofia@hotmail.com
        ajmi30001@yahoo.com
        alegmisofia@gmail.com
Cell: +218 91 4196843 (Tango).
SkyPe: ajmi.s

Presentation

Through my travels I noted that many worldwide people who I met were worried in deep, they have no clear ideas about (The big-knot), Them relationship with (The Life) and (The existence) mixed with scare, doubt, fables and falsity, many of them let themselves on the way of them parents without any debate, believed them and went out into the dark lonely, some of them took the shortcut-way to be an unbelievers, others lived them lives led by them enjoyments and selves pleasures, do not care about right and regular life, invalidated them minds as a rational beings, The blind instincts can do every sins with an inattentive minds.

All of them hid them misery behind false smiles.

Before long time I had swum in that misery pool, so I know them misery status!, and why?, the difference between I and them that was that I woke up early, and I searched for deep solution.

As a citizen of petroleum country I was rich, I had every wished things, but in my deep self I had felt unhappiness, my self had been burst, my soul wishes to fly in unknown perfect space.

I spent many years of my life learning and study everything about good relation -ship as a (human) with (The existence), (The Life),to save and control my life as a rational human-been, not as a miserable animal.

Most of people did not experienced the really happiness, they think that the happiness been by satisfy them (sex instinct) however, and comfortable life, but when they had or done that, they were found themselves in unhappiness status.

Money or sex or comfortable life don't make happiness, happiness been when you have a good and regulated relationship as (A Human) with (The existence) and (The Life), based on convinced mind and assuring heart.

I present you this window as a trying to help you to get your salvation way, but you do not forget that you are the master of your self, you can upgrade it to be better, controlled by your mind, or you can break down it, then you will be down of human status, nobody can be a deputy of you.

* Please note;
1- Here, I try here to short-cut for you a hundreds of Muslims philosophers articles wrote through many centuries used a perfect Arabic words and made many new idioms to many logical senses which did not found or been before, There is very difficult for everyone to translate its deep meanings, so Please use your full attention and

logical   sense to understand in deep what do I want to explain you!.
2- There is some repetition because there is many meanings overlapped with each others!.
                With my regards and love.

                        Alegmi Sofia
                        Tajoura - Libya
                        June 1 2013

The Big-Knot
The Human Relationship
with
The Existence and The Life

Through ages, The human has been searching for answers of those three important questions which are the base of his life center:
- *Who created him?*
- *Why?.*
- *What is his fate after death?.*

Human wants an answers, convince his mind and reassure his soul.

Greek philosophers, were the first people who had wrote about that human worry, the Greek philosopher Xenphanes, 560-478 BC who was agreed the theory of (The cosmos-union), humans thinking consolidated and redirected to esteem that (The cosmos) as is the God of the Beings and the life, that material view to the cosmos as (an union) that mean each of its parts completing each other to make in generally a cosmos-union which be the responsible of creating the existence and the life, that mean that it created itself from itself by itself, which is not permissible logically, (Material do not perishes or be from nonexistence*Darwin), also if he (the cosmos) is able to be creator that mean he had not been creating, and if he was created by other or by himself so he is not a the existence creator because he was an accident, limited by other power or by himself power in time and space, so not old, (older than the time and the place), if he is not old so he is not immortal (to be after time because he created in time as an accident that means there is previous before his creating he wasn't been yet), evanescent, never be the god, I will explain that in the following.

During the Christian middle centuries, many Muslims philosophers discussed that human think problem which nicknamed (The Big-knot), which be (A part of Islam culture, named – alone knowledge -) Averr(0)s - Ebn-Roshd- 1198-1226 analyzed and classified (The big-knot) in his philosophy books and enriched it, that (Big-Knot) problem killed many Muslim philosophers because before Ebn-Roshd coming there were many Muslims philosophers treated the Big-Knot, which has many logic complement steps sides to be known clearly as what I done here, the Muslims philosophers was did many metaphysical studies with some base mistakes led them to wrong logical results about human, cosmos, and life relationship, they killed by Muslims Sultans who they did not had a big minds to understand what those Muslims philosophers wanted to know *and explain in complex human subject?, and how they were enriched the human thinking for long time?, Ebn-Roshd found many subjects which connected were studied, he completed the empty and corrected the wrongs and enriched the poor, in the end reached a perfect logical solutions to many sides of (The Big-Knot).*

The Existence (The Reality)

The Muslims philosophers explained the reality in two parts:
1- The possible Reality.
2- The impossible Reality.

** The Possible reality.*
- The possible reality distributed in three parts:
1- Every things is under feeling of the five human-been senses, and tests, (Could been: seem, smelled, heard, touch, and tastes, like Milk, sun, earth, moon, .. est.).
2- Every things can human senses its appearance, like electricity, gravity, wind .. est.).
3- Every human mind can reach its results by logical way, like: calculation, logical thinking points, .. est.

** The Impossible reality.*
- It is every things or results over of human logical mind ability (over his senses feeling).

*   *Most of Materialists and all of Existentialism philosophers denied the impossible-reality, they explained the impossible-reality by an unconvinced materially explanation, based on hypothesis theories ground, and considered it as an impossible-reality, (Karl Markus, Charles Darwin, Heidegger Martin, est.),but they did not conceived that simple fact, that the human mind is limited (because he sensing the reality by limited senses) so it can not know or understand the unlimited, the metaphysical acts is completely out of our limitation, even whose had materially appearances.*

You can ask your self this simple question:

Why the Muslims philosophers made the impossible as (a realty) if it was not under human-been senses feeling or tests?

They made the impossible as (a reality) that means it is a fact, even if it is not been under human-been senses feeling or tests because:

1-They found the earth consisting: land, seas, and air, every part contains limited things as a parts, (trees, mountains, rivers), (everybody can touches its edges), then the earth must be limited because the total of limits become limited, as the total of millions of zeros will be zero no more, also, they concluded that the earth is a part of the cosmos (Earth, planets, suns, stars, space) and it is limited, so all cosmos must be limited, as what I said the total of limited become limited, therefore there is (Someone) made this cosmos, and because this cosmos are regulated and organized by secret complex totally program, so that (Someone) is a too rational-being has an unknown superpower, that (Unknown Rational Superpower being) who made this cosmos with all integrates must be (One) Just one, because every what he has done in same engineering plan, indicates to him as (one part) and (lonely), but this (Someone) is out of human-been mind senses or feeling, out of human rational limitation.

2- They found thousands of proofs indicate to unknown hidden things, can seem and known its effects, but none could knew its natures, as (The souls in the life bodies), The gravity, electricity, nucleus-power, human tested and controlled them appearances and built them modern civilization on its appearances acts powers, but really he couldn't knew its nature, clearly, some things or acts been runs out of human-been senses, do not subjugate to testing or control.

All that acts was a realty but it is in (Impossible) case.

The Truth

In Muslims philosophy there is two kinds of truths:

1) Logical truth.
2) Reported truth (based on logical truth).

The Logical truth.

Human been has a logical limited mind guides him to truth, that limited mind guiding his limited senses which been in limited body!.
- Human-been has a limited body, limited (cerebrum) has (some millions cells can be loaded), Limited force, and limited senses.

Then, logically you can say, that every truths ought to be limited, because it is done by a limited mind and senses.

Then, in practically fact, there is no unlimited truth been at all, because we can not understand unlimited truth as a fact by our limited minds, but we can going step by step under our limited minds and senses to understand.

The Reported Truth.

Reported truth is: Every reported or informed actions or effects built on bases of logical-truth.

If you were in your home balcony, in dark, and you saw a thief entered your home, that is a logical truth, because you saw him by your eyes, but if you were not in your home and your trusted neighbors informed you about that, then that is a (report-truth), because you based the information on (the trusting of your neighbors had!) basic, also if you found some human strange feet-prints effected on your empty house floor, then you should know that some one entered your home or made that effects through your absent.

The Thinking Operation

How is human been think?.

Muslims philosophers saw that human-been (thinking operation)prepares by three necessary data:
- Normal Human been Mind.
- Normal Human been senses.
- Previous information.

*The normal human mind using the previous information to make a judgment about every thing in your life, your (smell sense) smells flower and your eyes copies the picture of the flower and your hands touches it, your mind will save all that information as a previous information to use it in the future, if you find some flowers or something like it, your mind will give back you all that previous information to indicate you that this thing is as that flower you found before, or no, or there is any difference.

*The previous information been by two ways:

1- Tests and experiences information.
- Tests and experiences things by using your senses, and your previous information to make a judgment about everything.

2- Reported information.
-The learning and study books or notes of other people about any subject, that will charge your mind with reported information to use it as a previous information.

- Mind links the sense feeling with the previous information which saved about thing or action and give you a judgment to control your action, or to know that thing, if there is no previous information about that thing or action then it will try to make senses tests to directing you and stores all the information as a previous information to use in future.

Human-been structure

Muslims philosophies numerated the human structures in two parts:
1-Physical (body) needs.
2-Unphysical (The instincts).

1- The physical needs:

- Human physical have many needs like: Thirst, hunger, urine, food, drink, sleep … est.

* If human-been do not gratify or satisfy his physical needs will lead to death, and if he gratify or satisfy him body needs by wrong way he will be worry, as if he did not gratify or satisfy his unphysical (his instincts) by native right way.

2- The unphysical (The instincts):
Many of west and east philosophers denied the unphysical as a part of human-been structure, were been out of human laboratories tests, there is thousands of proofs indicate that they were in the wrong way.
- The human instincts is three, every instinct has many appearances leads human to be in certain act or behavior:
1- Religion instinct.
- Seem in acts or behavior as : pity, respect, worship, sacrificing, preference.. est.
2- Sex instinct.
- Seem in acts or behavior as : sex appeal, sex operation, fatherhood, motherhood, others been love, family love ..est.
3- (The staying) or to remain instinct.
- Seem in acts or behavior as: cowardice, fear, selfish, hypocrisy, self-defense, cunning, stinginess ..est.

If human did not gratify or satisfy his instincts appearances needs by native behavior or acts he will be worry himself and unhappy.

If Human-been do not controls and admin his physical and instincts needs and leads them to the right logical way will be backward himself to be in dark barbarian ages.

The limitation and un-limitation

The Limitation:

Muslims philosophers has explained the limited conditions is:

1) Everything has a beginning (commencement) or end or front or side or part or limit, can been under human senses.

Earth has limit, you can touch it, sun has a limit, you can see it, moon, stars, every thing has limits in certain body or picture or noise or space.

If you have too long rope rotated around the sun hundreds millions times and around all stars like that, then logically that rope has an end, and it is thing made by other higher than force made its limit.

2) Every limited is (a thing), needy, minus, occurred in limited time, time before its occurrence it was not, created by other higher that force made it, that means it was unavailable before certain time.

3) Every things are minus, needy, because it was made by other who made its limits, and it is not immortal because it is not old, made in certain time, before that certain time it wasn't been, it is an accidental (occurred in certain time will be limit to an end time).

* The un-limitation:
The un-limitation is everything been out of limited human mind perceive or understand, it is over than sensitive, no way to be under test or feeling, it is the complement of the minus of all things needs, it is old, been before time, immortal after time, not as any thing.

The big-Knot

History established facts about human behavior since the known history beginning, that human-been always adored something seemed great or strong or as an immortal thing, and let his imagination going away in illogical details as a mythological stories.

Human-been would be worry if he do not satisfy his Religion instinct which guided him to respect the full-power who produced and limited all his around things, he led by his religion instinct to did that.

Everybody, his religion instinct led him to respect and adored something as his government, money, life, power, force, moneyed people, himself, ..est., if he did not directs his religion instinct to the right direction, he will fall in lies swamp, out of human logical basic.

This direction named by the Muslims philosophers (The big knot), because it is the crossroads in human-been is life, if he chooses the right way then he will be fine and happy, but if he made a mistake choosing he will be faraway without farewell.

His choice will formed his behavior and actions in certain form along his life, then people must be-careful to do not takes the wrong way.

Do we need a God been in our Life?

Since history dawn the Human-been led by his religion instinct search for many answers of his logic mind questions, he wants know the full power who produced the cosmos, he found everything led by a good system, he could not imagined that this cosmos made by chance!, no sane one can believes that the chance or an accident can does all that incredible automatism system for everything, then who did that?, and why he is hidden?, and how he can reach him?.

Because Human-been is limited, so always he is going to the perfection to completes his minus, worldwide people wish perfection in every thing, perfect statue or paint will stop them walk to enjoy them eyes and wondered for them human brother act, every perfection in any way, in work, producing and arts has longing, respect, attraction to who done it.

Human is a minus, needy, needs complete, loves and wishes perfection and he obligates by act made in his nature as a natural behavior to attracting the perfection, he saw the perfection in any natural thing around him, so he wishes to be a part from that perfection, he led by his (Religion instinct) to respect and adore that perfection done, but the specification of that (perfect-being) is under impossible-truth, then he can not reach him by any way.

Someone from Arabian Bedouin lived before Islam coming said: (when I found a camel dung I know that it were a camel came to this way, so large land has large space and sky has zodiacs do not indicate to the master !).

Muslims philosophers esteemed that the human-been is the known sane being in the land, then he is the lonely qualified to drive the life in the earth, but he has a limited senses, mind, and force, his limitation takes him far of perfection status, so the god must had a perfection properties, human mind can not imagine it with easy because it is over his perceive, because the perfection can breed limited being (fail, short, minus), but limited being can not breed the perfection.

They concluded that the god must have a perfection specification incompatible with the human-been limitation specification:

1- Must be (lonely), unlimited.

- Because when he is more than one he will limit by the other, so he is a limited thing, so he is minus, needy, that he does not make him a god!

2- Must be (an old) been before time and he must be after time (an Immortal).

- Because all things propped to him.

3- Must be perfect in any way, for any subject.

- Do Not needy thing, because he is the source of the existence, so he must rich than the existence, can complete every minus of beings or things.

4- He has a free will, has not behavior, purpose, usually, do not sleep or asleep, do not inattention.

5- He must have full-power to care and do every thing in his kingdom in same time.

* Human-been worshipped many limited things as sun, moon, stars, cows, or natural phenomenon as volcanoes, waterfalls, even trees, seas, mountains, every thing seemed as an

impossible full power (the God) who bred the cosmos and the life.

The God

The God sent hundreds of human messengers and prophets from time to time to the earth rudder through hundreds of centuries to learn them the truth about him, and the right way for them life, but after short time of god messenger depart, often times, human forgot and fell down to dark life again.

Allah

(Allah)was unknown and unclear name before Islam came 1433 years ago, Arabs was listened this name from unknown part, perhaps by (Ishmael) son of Abraham who rebuilt (the Kaaba), the Allah home in land before long centuries ago from Islam came by (Mohammed) The Islam prophet, They were learned the name of the god was (Allah).

Who is Allah?

The god (Allah) presented himself in Koran in nice and perfect eloquent words never human can did it, which means: (Allah) is only one, present, never had been bore or born, never someone or thing had fit him, or similar him, he is been in anytime, everywhere, he is near

everybody, sees and hears everything, know everything, close or open, older than everything, everything has end but him.), so this presentation agreeing with the human-been logical (the impossible-truth) theory result.

In the beginning, Arabs did not understood in deep those little eloquent words, but after some time came, some philosophers had big minds ready to knew the secret of that little words.

Mohammed

In middle of the sixth century someone illiterate, forty years old, has a good reputation, nicknamed - The Honest -, named Mohammed came from mountain cave near Makkah which been in middle of Arab peninsula declared that he is the last God messenger and prophet, came with the God speaking to all worldwide people to guide them to the right way.

Most of people worldwide knows the god, as a god of the cosmos and the life, but they deny Mohammed as a prophet and messenger of the god (Allah)!.

Was Mohammed a liar?

History told everybody that Mohammed had many materially miracles as a proofs of his declaration, but his big proof was The Koran book, so, what is the Koran book?, is it The God speaking book or no?

Makkah refusal reasons :

From the beginning Makkah the rich bourgeoisie society denied Mohammed as a God prophet for this reasons:

1- Makkah has (Kaaba) (the Allah holy house) which Arabians coming to it for hajj, hajj bred a large commerce earns a large profit for all Makkah people (specially the bourgeoisie), and big traders, so the new Mohammed (hidden lonely God) religion will break them large market, from other side them rank and influence as a leaders of idolatry religion of all Arabian idolaters of Arab peninsula will be break down.

2- He was a lonely poor man (not bourgeois one), and not a member of them drunk club, he was has not wished them corruption, vice, drunk, nude.

Makkah did not denied his personality as a perfect man, before his prophecy declaration was nicknamed him - The honest -, as a trusted man, the keeper of them deposits for tens years, then how changed all that respect status for him to denial status?, it is the selfish advantage, Mohammed prophecy was against them materially and un-materially advantage.

Other people refusal reasons:

Other persons denied Mohammed were haughty people, history told us about them excuses:

* Magic, charm:

Reader knows that the Arabians before Islam were the first and last people in the history made a yearly (Eloquence talk contest), named (Oukath-Market) held every eloquent poet, all eloquences people come yearly from all Arab peninsula to (Oukath market) to listen to eloquent Arabic talk, and there is many Arabians judges gave an judgments about what they were heard or read, ten long eloquence poems were hung into Kaaba, they were the top eloquence poems in Arabic language in the known history, so Arabians knew the deep of the Arabic language very well, So they are understood that the Koran language is a perfect over than any human eloquence language been even the top ten poems which hung in Kaaba, for that, they did not know the source of that words, them eloquence indicated to the fact, that those words was not a human words, no one can say like that, a words make them in other status, opens them eyes in an intimate world, all of it is white, peaceful, merciful and clear, never they had saw or heard like this talking before, they knew how is

Mohammed talking been, he was not a poet or eloquent, they can easily notes the difference between Mohammed talk, and his Koran talk, for that, they accused him (Magic), (charm) as an excuses to deny him, but they knew him very well, he never was a magician or juggler, he was the same man who known.

* Materially miracles:

Some people requested Mohammed to bring angels been with him, or to have a gold palaces contains gardens, waterfalls and rivers, others requested him to see Allah by eyes and touch him by hands.
.

* You can note that every miracles requested from some people was a materially miracles uses to pride and haughty been, Koran had many replies for preach and remember them about.

* Mohammed had miracles everyday, but they did not been declared, just who near him in that moment could see, or who it may concern, but his big miracle is the Koran, who is near us by its easily and far of us by its secrets.

The Holy Koran

Koran is not like some other holy books because the first published copy of Koran was collected and wrote in one big book contained All Koran speaking, there were an identically copy, which been yet now, no lonely comma or word were lost, or not clear, it was directly form Allah by his Angel messenger Mr. Gabriel to Mohamed wrote in five books, no more no less, sent to the four land directions after few years of Mohammed is death.

* Was the Koran created by Mohammed himself?

In the beginning of Mohamed prophecy, the contemporary Arabians did not counseled Koran was created by Mohammed himself, because it was clear for them the difference between his talk and Koran, the Arabic eloquence known forbade them to say that, but they suggest that it was created by unknown high power as (magic, priestly), none said that Mohammad created or he can create like that words, the Romanians of that time who did not understood the Arabic language eloquence when they informed that the Koran is impossible thing done, they sent someone to inform Makkah people that (some-one Romanian) *is the really author of Koran!, but that is seem as a joke, because if the Arabs eloquent could not did it, and they agreed that no body could did it, so how someone Romanian could did it?, and gave it to Mohammed!, the Romanians tried to do some false noise.*

* In old Arabian culture Koran was the top honor thing, if Mohammed declared that he was the author of Koran so he should been the king of all The Arab peninsula, but he declared in simply that this honorable book created by (Other one) and he was just a messenger of that (Other one).

* Many Koran (Aayat) - articles - were chides and menaced Mohammed himself, and criticized some of his acts, who was created book contain full sections against himself?

* Every creators excused them readers or listeners for any mistakes or faults in them articles or speaks, but Koran did not, Koran challenged everybody through ages to do articles like Koran, Koran said that never being can do that, if all peoples united with all demons never can do it, said that with decisive words.

At The Koran challenge time, the old world wondered, no creator challenged all worldwide humans and Jinn to did as him speaking, through history centuries.

Many unbelievers people tried to did speaks as Koran, but they couldn't did that, they created some dead words.

* Koran and Mohammed informed people of that time for many future acts happened after that.

* Koran indicated to many science facts did not known in that time as -the earth Globular- the air pressure -, Christians height in the present-life, the human creating in his mother womb!, call wave killing living beings!, power of atoms, and explained many very old believers and unbelievers people stories and indicated to them graved cities, many medicines made by Koran indications.

* Now, Computer shows us some of the Koran secrets, it was difficult for human counting, how could created a book through 23 years contains secrets shown year by year?, how he could calculated the words in his speak through 23 years?

* Please Look these some examples about some words which repeated in Koran:

The present-life 115 times. - The After-life 115 times.

The Angel 88 times - The Satan 88 times.

Life 145 times - Death 145 times.

Man (n) 24 times - Woman 24 times.

The Devil 11 times - Refuge from Devil 11 times.

Useful(adj) 50 times - Decay (n)50 times.

Desire (n) 8 times - Awe (n)8 times.

Misfortune 75 times - Thank 75 times.

alms-giving 32 times - Blessing 32 times.

Distress(n) 114 times. - Patient (adj)114

Mohammed 4 times. - Islam Law 4 times.

Day 365 times. - (A year has 365 days).

Month 12 times. - (A year has 12 months).

Prayer 5 times. - (The daily Islam prayers is five at five times).

* Koran said which means: (Allah has in his hand the (forelocks) of every created), and in other position said which means: (… If he did not stop we will burn his forelock, liar, misdeed forelock!), Muslims didn't understood what was he meant through centuries, some years ago Canadian scientist found a proof that the front of human cerebrum (human forelock) is the responsible of human willpower to do lie and missed, if this front part of human cerebrum cut or burnt then human lost his willpower to lie and to make misdeed acts.

There is many proofs indicated that, the Koran didn't created by Mohammed himself and it isn't a charm or magic been.

The Islam

(Islam) word means in Arabic Language nearly of this English sentences meaning (Surrender with peaceful), or (surrendered the self to Allah with peace and salute).

* Islam*:*

Islam is (For everybody), has five corners:
1- Believing in Allah as a lonely God of existence, human-been, and life, and, Mohammed is a God slave and his messenger.
2- Daily five prayers.
3- Hajj to Makkah one time in a life.
4- Fasting Ramadan month.
5- Giving Almsgiving to poor people.

* Eaman (Belief):

Eaman is a high degree of Islam status, for people who put themselves in order of Allah in deep details, make good more than others.

Those people more than others be exposed to ordeals.

In Islam culture the Present-life is a short trip passing to the hereafter-life, Allah do not gives a reward to who believes Mohammed in the present-life, his rewards will be in hereafter-life.

Who become Muslim will feel a new happiness, peace and calm in his difficult new life because often he will be in more ordeals in his present-life.

The present-life is completely for the unbelievers people,(Every selves wishing: Pride, Rich, Material, force, power ..est.).

Allah said in Koran which means: (Do you want enter paradise without (be in ordeals? - been in tests - to establish arguments to liars and honest people), then when you want Allah esteems you as a believer then you must make you self ready for many proofs examinations through your life, this tests will let you know your belief level in every your life fields.

See those two examples, one by Allah (in Koran) other by Mohammed.
* - Koran said which means: (We wish to do for every unbelievers a silver roofs to them homes and stairs to ascend up)!.

That talk means, that Allah seemed as he encourages people to unbelieving for him and his messenger!.

* Someone came to Mohammed and told him: (Mohammed, the Allah Messenger, I love Allah, and I love you!), Mohammed replayed him which

means: (*If you love Allah deeply I presage you to be in ordeals, If you love me in deep I presage you will be poor and sorrowful).*

You can not boast that you love Allah and his messenger in deep or in special case more than others without paying cost.

Mr. Gabriel the Allah special Angel messenger told Mohammed that he was there when Allah created (The Paradise) and (The Fire), and he was afraid when he saw Allah made all human enjoyments, pleasures, delights and every human-been selves wish and love in fire ways, and made every human-been self hardship, unwished, ordeals, in the paradise ways, when Mohammed retold that to his Muslims companions, they cried as children!.

*Koran said in other positions as a warning to people which means:(Do you think that we were created you to play?), and (We can made every land redder been believers!) (You are the poor one but Allah is the rich one ..) (If you believed for Allah you would not make Allah rich, if you did not, you wouldn't make Allah poor!) (If everybody, or beings, humans and Jinn, who dead and in life come together as one plane to benefit Allah, they can't, or to harm him, they can't), (If you make the seas ink and all land trees pens, to write Allah knowledge, you cant!), (You can not make you lovers been believers, Allah guides who

wants!), (If you don't content with my fate and orders, so make a tunnel in the earth or ascend in sky!).

Termination

Now you have all main information about every sides of - The Big-Knot - Islam solution in shortly, now you need to gave yourself a chance to be better, and lead your self to be in orders of Allah and his Messenger, and avoid evil which out of them order, you will feel a new life happiness, you will touch the peace covered you, and there is a special care for you in any life difficulty objects your way, If you be faithful so some more difficult happens will be in your way, but in any status you will be full happy in secret, request Allah to care, help, and bless you.

__ End ___

Author books صدر للمؤلف
****
1 دراسات Studies

1- الاستخبارات العسكرية ـ تطبيق إداري معاصر ـ (ج 1).

2- الاستخبارات العسكرية ـ عمليات الميدان - (ج 2).

3- (The Big Knot).

4- (العقدة الكبرى) – ترجمـة لكتـاب The Big Knot).

5- (حصافة 2012-2013) مجموعة مقالات حصافة.

2 روايـــات Novels

1- (صديقتي الفرنسية)(My French Girlfriend).

2- (عاد مع الريح) (Came back with wind).

3- (انتقام الأبرياء) (Innocents Revenge).

4- (That is what the stone said!).

5- (Runaway to The West).

6- (Born against Government).

7- (Bullet in Darkness).

8- (From notebook of Apostate).

9- (A Man from The Middle-East).

10- (On Europe Steps).

11- (A Story has a beginning).

12- (The Last Man).

13- (A Muslim In our house).

www.ingramcontent.com/pod-product-compliance
Lightning Source LLC
Chambersburg PA
CBHW041804040426
42448CB00001B/32